TWISTERS

NOISY BOOKS

Paul Harrison
and Fabiano Fiorin

Evans

I love the
quiet library.

And all its noisy books.

"ROAR!" goes the dinosaur.

"Shh!" says Mum.

10

"BOOM!" goes the cannon.

"Shh!" says Mum.

15

"WHOO!" goes the ghost.

16

"Shh!" says Mum.

"ZAP!" goes the alien.

"Shh!" says Mum.

Home time.

"WHOOPS!" goes Mum.

"THUD" go the books.

"Shh!" I say.

31

Why not try reading another Twisters book?

Not-so-silly Sausage by Stella Gurney and Liz Million 978 0237 52875 1

Nick's Birthday by Jane Oliver and Silvia Raga 978 0237 52896 6

Out Went Sam by Nick Turpin and Barbara Nascimbeni 978 0237 52894 2

Yummy Scrummy by Paul Harrison and Belinda Worsley 978 0237 52876 8

Squelch! by Kay Woodward and Stefania Colnaghi 978 0237 52895 9

Sally Sails the Seas by Stella Gurney and Belinda Worsely 978 0237 52893 5

Billy on the Ball by Paul Harrison and Silvia Raga 978 0237 52926 0

Countdown by Kay Woodward and Ofra Amit 978 0237 52927 7

One Wet Welly by Gill Matthews and Belinda Worsley 978 0237 52928 4

Sand Dragon by Su Swallow and Silvia Raga 978 0237 52929 1

Cave-baby and the Mammoth by Vivian French and Lisa Williams 978 0237 52931 4

Albert Liked Ladders by Su Swallow and Tim Archbold 978 0237 52930 7

Molly is New by Nick Turpin and Silvia Raga 978 0237 53067 9

A Head Full of Stories by Su Swallow and Tim Archbold 978 0237 53069 3

Elephant Rides Again by Paul Harrison and Liz Million 978 0237 53073 0

Bird Watch by Su Swallow and Simona Dimitri 978 0237 53071 6

Pip Likes Snow by Lynne Rickards and Belinda Worsely 978 0237 53075 4

How to Build a House by Nick Turpin and Barbara Nascimbeni 978 0237 53065 5

Hattie the Dancing Hippo by Jillian Powell and Emma Dodson 978 0237 53335 9

Mary Had a Dinosaur by Eileen Browne and Ruth Rivers 978 0237 53337 3

When I Was a Baby by Madeline Goodey and Amy Brown 978 0237 53334 2

Will's Boomerang by Stella Gurney and Stefania Colnaghi 978 0237 53336 6

Birthday Boy by Dereen Taylor and Ruth Rivers 978 0237 53469 1

Mr Bickle and the Ghost by Stella Gurney and Silvia Raga 978 0237 53465 3

Noisy Books by Paul Harrison and Fabiano Fiorin 978 0237 53467 7

Undersea Adventure by Paul Harrison and Barbara Nascimbeni 978 0237 53463 9

For John Joe and Sam – PH

First published 2007
Evans Brothers Limited
2A Portman Mansions
Chiltern Street
London W1U 6NR

Text copyright © Paul Harrison 2007
© in the illustrations Evans Brothers Limited 2007

British Library Cataloguing in Publication Data

Harrison, Paul, 1969-
    Noisy books. - (Twisters)
    1. Children's stories
    I. Title
    823.9'2[J]

ISBN: 978 0237 53468 4 (hb)
ISBN: 978 0237 53467 7 (pb)

Printed in China

Series Editor: Nick Turpin
Design: Robert Walster
Production: Jenny Mulvanny

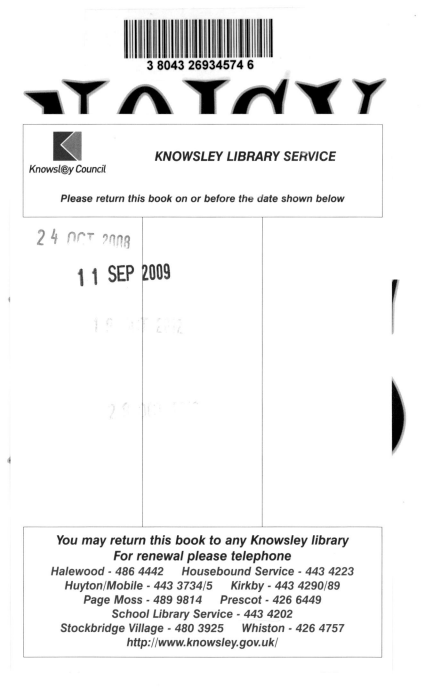